SELCOUTH CLISHMACLAVER

or: *Dancing with Strangers and Their Friends*

A Zinger Publications Book
Published by Zinger Publications of Zinger Media Group LLC

Copyright © 2015 by Isaiah M. Williams

All rights reserved. No part of this publication may be reproduced, stored in any form of retrieval system, or transmitted in any form or by any means electronic, mechanical, photocopying, recording or otherwise without the express written permission of the publisher.

Zinger Publications is a registered trademark of Zinger Media Group LLC.

Printed in the United States of America

ISBN 978-0-692-36290-7

Published for print and e-book by:
Zinger Publications – A Zinger Media Group Venture
www.ZingerMediaGroup.com
Cleveland, Ohio

SELCOUTH CLISHMACLAVER

The Second *Collection* of "Poetry" by
Isaiah M. Williams

ALSO BY ISAIAH M. WILLIAMS
Eclecticism Vol. 1
Power Walker (forthcoming)

For Mary

"Don't read too much into it."
—Unknown

SELCOUTH CLISHMACLAVER

part one: story of one

INTRO

I went a little off the rails
With this one.
So much so that the
Introduction is a poem
Itself, thought of by me
While I was writing it.
That, is poetry, you see.
Writing as you think;
Thinking as you write,
Not really thinking about
What you write,
But still thinking
Probably about how shitty
Your life is or how in love
You are with the idea of
Being in love with someone,
Or constructing prose with
Forced rhymes and schemes
Of A, A, B, B or A, B, A, B,
The usual probably.
As I write this, I think
Of how many complaints
I have about prose and poetry
And literature in general,
But I still write this indeed,
Complicit.
I went a little off the rails
With this one,
Probably similar to how
You once fathomed a Tyler Durden,

Your own Tyler Durden,
Maybe it was a *Durdenesque* thought,
Maybe named something else,
Like contemplation
But still a Tyler.
Still a Tyler, who tells
You that you've conformed,
That you're a machine,
With a machine mind,
Which by the way really isn't
A mind
If you think about it,
But a part of a machine
That is still a machine,
Even when it dies.
Who reads poetry?
I can tell you.
The dreamers do,
Poets do,
And that's about it
Probably because poetry
Is the least respected art form.
But what I've presented here is not art;
Instead, it's regurgitation,
Which some would call art,
And I would just call it disgusting.
I've fathomed a Tyler Durden,
And that Tyler told me to write
This.
Not this introduction

In particular, but this book
Of me, of my Tyler Durden.
This descent, which proceeds
In the coming pages, will define
Me, and maybe even define you.
But I don't care about that,
I care about your mind.
Yes, you.
I care about your mind.
I've been told I'm too
Didactic in my writing,
So this one is about
Me.
It's about how I've learned
To teach myself
The things I've wanted to
Teach others about themselves.
I've been alone too long with
My own thoughts about
What your thoughts may be
As a reader of poetry.
I've asked myself questions
In the third person hoping
To get to the second person,
While ignoring the first person.
Take what is here, in these pages,
And ignore the structure
Because there is not one.
I want your Tyler to read
This book, and tell you

About what you read
And if after that you still
Want to shoot your Tyler
In the head,
Do it.

part two: i listen to me

"ARE YOU LISTENING?"

I am trepidatious to use the word *you* in my writing of poetry just
As I am afraid to press enter on the keyboard because of what
Message might be sent by the space in between the stanzas and
How many lines are in each one, and because of what *you* might
Mean to some people, and what *you* might mean to me.

The space in between these stanzas is to me more important than
The words that surround them because I can think of no greater
Thing than nothingness and I can think of no greater feeling than
What I've been given by you and no greater yearning than to revert
What you were to me back to nothingness.

I give thought to writing just as you gave thought to what you
Actually said to me the day that you told me I should listen
Because your mother had gotten sick and you had to give away
Your dog and your dream school was beginning to seem more and
More far fetched as your mother got sicker and as you started to
Miss your dog more and as your grades slipped through your grasp
On life as you knew it.

You reminded me how you would always take the walk between us
And I would think about how stupid I was to let you do that
Knowing that I could have easily done the same thing to show my
Fondness of you as opposed to what was done upon arrival.

Now I reminisce as I look through all the sorted letters of our
Youth, not the youth I currently experience, but the youth of my
Mind and how stupid I was to let you do the things I did, go the
Places I went, and see the things I saw.

I fret at the idea of seeing you again, as now it has been three years,
But I text you regularly; ah, I think about what technology has
Done to my communication skills, or perhaps how it stifled or
Jumpstarted whatever I didn't have of communication skills and
Talking to you has become easier because I don't know you
Anymore.

I know what your timeline tells me and what your feed feeds me,
But I know nothing more because you've changed just as your
Heresy has become faith and your tolerance has become
Intolerance and your love has become thwarted and your
Expressions have become of grief to a foreign deity or god or
Something and your glasses have become bigger on your face.

I've realized I am drawn to people who are smarter than I am or
Who appear to be smarter than I think I appear to others to be,
And perhaps this the reason why I was so drawn to you and what
You would do and whom you would talk to and whom you would
Hang around just as I wanted to talk to you and hang around you.

So maybe *I* am *you* or at least just like you, and to think of it, that
Situation wouldn't be all too bad because you're not too bad, or at
Least the you I knew three years ago wasn't too bad, and I wish
That you could be the three-years-ago-you again, but that is
Unreasonable because I am no longer the three-years-ago-me
Either.

Through you I've realized that yearning for nothing is actually
Yearning for something because that something is for you to
Become nothing to me, *but* I've become indifferent towards the

Fact that you will always be something, never nothing, as I am to You.

I take responsibility for what happened to you, as you've told me I Should, but I still can't fathom a thought as to why you'd allow it Just as I did.

SATIRE

I live, a satire.

No, I do not live a satire,
But I live, a satire.

I hold up to ridicule
Follies, vices, and shortcomings
To shame people
Into improvement.

I take myself seriously too, as if to poke fun at others in order to
Make them feel aware of their shortcomings, and I assume that
They weren't aware already; of course it's audacious and
Unwarranted and unqualified, but what would I have to offer
Others besides criticism that I have designed and intended to be
Totally constructive and to be totally others' faults when they take
It the wrong way?

How else could I feel important?

How else would I make sure there was some measurable for my
Impact on others' lives such as their reactions to *my* input?

How else could I feel needed externally?

I mean, I am criticized at all wakes and efforts and opportunities,
So it is not much more than the result of my training and
Engineering and manufacturing that I criticize and bring attention
To others' shortcomings, a satire.

POEM

"A poem is the only place were an editing mistake or typoe alike is
Allowed, the only place where you can scream without your voice,
Run without your legs, and cry without looking like a child," I
Think.

I drink coffee from behind or in front of the computer screen,
Which is my newspaper at the moment and ignore the school
Beyond the window.

Dormant halls wait out the weekend before dread creeps in five
Minutes earlier than the bell should ring.

This is not a morning to remember, as spring teased the week prior
With soft, earnest hands, though again winter asserted its icy
Influence until I was left with a nameless landscape—a white sheet
Draped over the drive in, encircled by disdain, and leaving me
Waiting for the waltz, the foxtrot, and all the other dances to stop
So that I could join in.

Not a morning compelling enough to grab for even what must be
Next, so I scroll from one icon and headline to the next and find
Nothing, for then I set out for the day to achieve nothing short of
Nothing.

APOLOGIA

I called it a shadow after each night,
with either of us,
and I unfastened its drawstring,
considered our complaints,
added to its size,
denied myself those attitudes,
and denied you the
satisfaction of knowing I tried to change.

PATH

I keep watching science fiction shows on a history channel lately,
First wondering why the shows show on a history channel and then
Thinking about space, and although what little I know about
Science says curtly that its equivalent fiction bears less resemblance
To science than fiction, I still imagine that my own fiction, of
Gravity, which is slightly greater than zero, is a greater daydream
Now than those youth gave *because* I imagine the stability that a
Minuscule, dragging orbit could offer well enough to outdo the
Still, lesser, orbit of conjecturing.

WELL, SHIT

I dropped my phone in the toilet
The other day,
Postpartum of course,
And it made me think about how
Shitty everything is.

I stayed calm though,
But before I could think,
I was wrist deep in a probably
Unidentifiable substance to recover it.

Then I thought to myself,
"I'm sick of this shit."

WUNDERKIND

I imagine a busy lobby
Filled with virtuoso musicians.
They're probably here for
A convention or something.
They're independent, though.

Not one orchestra.
Not working together.
Independent.
They've tuned their instruments,
And practiced their pieces.

They look at each other.
The pianists to the percussionists.
Might I point out
There aren't pianists on pianos.
They have keyboards.
Because that's more practical.
The flutists to the clarinetists.

I watch them intently.
I'm not a musician though.
I think, "Why are there so many?"
I refer to the musicians probably.

As if on cue
They all begin to play,
At once.
Their own pieces.
At once.

I hear this blunderbuss of noise.
It makes no sense at first.

Pianists play low notes,
And percussionists do their thing.

Flutists blow me away,
And clarinetists play high.
They play so well.

Individually, though.

I can listen to them individually
And all at once.

The music gets better as time
Goes on.

They cancel each other out.

I hear nothing.

part three: welcome aboard

CYNIC

I distrust most people, and I'm not sure
Why cynicism gets such a bad rep.
I'm told it's bad to be selfish.
That's pretty messed up.

I embrace my cynicism.
Physically, I do.
Like it's a baby or a puppy
Or a short poem.

LOAFERS

I think of lovers.
Young lovers,
Starbucks lovers,
Who stare at one another,
An open notebook on the table,
No coffee yet.
At some point,
They'll order the other's drink
And ask the poor barista
To put hearts next to
The swirly handwriting
Of a name that will
One day be forgotten
Just like this love.
They'll chuckle at it.
I think of how content
They must be with
Discontentment.
And how filled they'll be
With caffeine and yearning.
I sit in this Starbucks
With my sugary coffee
And watch them,
Not them.

I ONCE CALLED MYSELF A SHARK AND IT BACKFIRED

I think now of the noisiness of
My quiet mornings.
I've been told I sleep too little;
I tell myself I sleep too little.

I give a shove to the comfort
Of mediocrity and get up at
Half past five.
I say hi to Giene and
Leave.

The darkness of my drive in
Makes me think of
Death.
And taxes.
And self-interest.
Life's three guarantees.

Once I thought,
"What if you are still conscious
After death?
And that's it.
You are just conscious,
Trapped,
In your mind,

Forever, not having
Any new stimuli,
Forever, contending with
Whatever memories you may

Have had during
Life."
There are many evolutionary
Flauws.

And my drive in is one of them.

part four: toward reality

IT'S BAD LUCK TO BREAK A CLOCK

I never have time for me.
Or maybe I do, but spend
That time thinking about how
I never have time for me.

Maybe if I die
I'll have the time to finally
Isolate
The true version of myself
Untainted by worldly inducements.

Sounds a lot like heaven to me.
Maybe.
Perhaps, I'll get control for all the
Variables
To see the effect of me on me.

I think about how I live mostly,
My mind bouncing around
All day going from one screwed up thought
To another,
Never being mindful of the world around
Me.

I don't live in reality anyway.

ACTUAL DREAMS I'VE HAD

1. I was Jules Winnfield expressing
How I had a moment
Of clarity
As if I was an alcoholic
Who had had one
And was now Jules telling Vincent
About my proud moment.

2. I was in a backseat of an Oldsmobile with
Kevin Bacon talking about
Existentialism.

3. I was typing a message
To a girl friend without
Moving my fingers, then I felt
That it was just a dream, so I turned
Off the phone, but the light would
Not go out.

4. I was inconsolable
Because of the lack of responses
From my Tinder matches
To my typical "Hey."

5. I asked a Victorian woman
Who stood in front of an old building
On a street I didn't know
About how long it took to get over heartbreak
And I didn't quite understand
Her answer, but it was probably

"A long time."

part five: dancing with strangers

SOME HAIKUS

1. *I* am a haiku;
My being is a template,
A contribution.

2. I give the effort,
The outsiders will complain;
You will bring the pain.

3. Comedy is tough,
So is making people laugh;
They are not the same.

HIM

I am an extension
Of the apprehension
Of her.

I am the result
Of her life's tumult,
And I remind her of that.

My looks remind her of his,
But that's not all it is
Because she can't remember his face.

VOICEMAIL

I've always struggled in my scholarly study of greetings or
Salutations or whatever the hell those things are called that you
Hear when someone conscientiously ignores your phone calls
Probably by pressing ignore or just staring at it until it stops in the
Hopes that you won't know that they ignored it because it didn't
Immediately go to voicemail.

Should I say, "Have a *great* day," at the end? I mean I wouldn't
Want the asshole who watched his or her phone ring after I
Mustered the courage to put my weird-sounding-telephone-voice
To their ear to tell me to have a great day let alone tell me what the
Hell to do at all.

Then there's always, "Have a *blessed* day." Yeah, that's the über
Religious one that everyone gets weird about once they hear it
Assuming that the person who recorded it is waiting in a dark
Corner of their home waiting to jump out and beat them with a
Bible or stand over them while they sleep to smother them with
The holy white pillow of scripture.

"Take care." Although I am fond of Drake and his indulgence in
The hyperbole and his ability to make even the solidest of men
Miss their first love, what exactly will the listener be taking care of?
Again, telling someone what to do is never a good idea especially
When that person is probably pissed already that you didn't answer
The phone.

"Talk to you later." Will you? Will you talk to me later? Because it
Appears that you just ignored my call. Do you even want to talk to

Me? I mean, there is the off chance that someone legitimately
Missed your call instead of ignoring it, but not really.

The worst is the default, the norm, the first one, the "You are
Attempting to contact someone who has a voice mailbox that has
Not been set up yet," bullshit that lazy people never know exists
Until some fed up person tells them about their bullshit that is
Their laziness and that is their lack of effort to set up their voice
Mailbox on a phone they got about a year ago.

I often think about how I would break *my* norm and my truth and
My values and my morals and my fiber to call you on the phone to
Hear your voice, to hear you breathe, to be weird with you, but
You would not answer, so I was stuck listening to the robot that
Was your default recording.

It was probably default because you were unoriginal in your own
Original way. At least you weren't lazy and you put in some effort
To and set up your mailbox. You were still a robot though—you're
Voicemail was not a recording of you, but a of a robot that was
Representing you, resenting me.

Did you receive the calls that I made in a haze to you on the hopes
That perhaps you would answer after I'd already told you off the
Day before causing you to hang up on me and me to hang my
Head low regretting what I'd just done, not what I'd just said?

part six: and their friends

MY FRIENDS WILL NEVER READ MY POEMS

Remember that time when we wanted to watch a movie,
Probably the last thing I wanted to do at that moment,
But you bought *The 40-Year-Old Virgin* electronically and you
Played it but paused it and it was paused so long that your TV got
Burn-in while we carried on revealing conversations that lasted for
Hours into the next morning?

ORDINARY

One risk at a time, bright and hot, everywhere else invisible,
As a fortified instinct to hold and keep splits in half into a before
And after.

Living in dissimilar light, the pull of shadows, mess and noise,
As this world is shared willfully, I say ordinary takes time.

SOUNDS LIKE A BOMB

"Sounds like a bomb," one of us said.
Our guide points across the tide, over shrubby aromatic North
American plants of the daisy family and the hills they sit on.
We stand quiet for a while and feel the percussion interrupting the
Drone of tires on the interstate highway.
We hear jet boats on the lake blasting against the current,
The constant buzz of hydropower crackling in transmission lines
Overhead.
We're on the enclosure for experimentation, where science knocks
Apart the building blocks of everything, fanning emotional and
Atomic blaze enough to vaporize us all.
"But let us not think about that," our guide says.
He wants us to enjoy the sunshine, get comfortable.

POETS

For even considering the idea of the idea to even put what they do down on paper, romancing that idea and then courting it into journals or magazines or chapbooks, using them and allowing them to be saved in chronicles and put up on fridges; for stirring nostalgia, a witch's brew filled with new words and phrases that do not connect or make sense if read in different tones, and do not bring promise, do not offer warm feeling or make you stand up on a table and dance like Helen of Troy, I thank you.

THIS WEEK'S END

I've decided to spend the weekend shooting unusual words from
My backside like blood underneath a stitch but hopefully without
The need for tan bedpans and soggy messes.

I will talk about Mars and sing Elton John and eat too much pizza
And then justify it by comparing the number of pieces I ate to the
Number of pieces that my skinny friends ate.

I will meet someone whose existence is close enough to that of
Someone who I have wanted to meet for three years, and I will tell
Her I am crazy about her, and then I will Google what that phrase
Means to make sure that I have used it correctly.

THE ARCHIVE

As if in some sort of archival system, I keep all of our text messages,
To look for fun sometimes at the evolution of what some might
Call a friendship, but I would call weird.

I use the word weird as if to confer my personal judgment on the
Whole mess and to describe what we were, what we are, and what
We always will be, especially once we see each other again after a
Very short break, but to prepare for which we thought of each
Other, or at least I thought of you, and I thought of you perhaps
Thinking of me.

CLEAR

I'm composed fine,
Results of minutes before clear,
Everything else not so much so.
I'm so tall that I claim your driveway.
I'm a dancer in a circle of screamers,
And I scream with them.

I meet people with very
American hearts;
They're mid-sized
And comfortable.

Hello.

PROGRESS [ION]

It is often very easy to forget our background and mislabel our Privilege.

I have lost the ability to tell whether or not what I am feeling and Experiencing and wading through is progression or whether or not I am just getting used to my current condition.

So I'll just label [mis]label it: progression.

Not progress, but progression.

CLISHMACLAVER

I wake again, again; five hours after I fell asleep at once, I wake
Again.

I wake again with an indifferent disposition, a disposition that to
This day, to this interruption of five heavy hours of sleep, has
Stifled me because I cognize and recognize it as innate.

This innateness I cognize as engineering, perhaps social, so it is not
My place to question or alter it.

PSYCHO OR: PSYCHIC

I subscribe to the ideology that my time here can be spent in any
Way that I wish to spend it, thank you very much.

My friends barely recognize me anymore, or at least that's what I
Think, and to tell the truth, I barely recognize them anymore
Either.

No, not certain friends in particular, but the entire notion of
Friends and what my choice of friends might perhaps say about me
And my choices on the whole.

Perhaps I look forward to fresh starts.

Unfortunately I know that as I grow older, the programmed,
Destined, fresh starts will start to expire and run out and I will be
Responsible for designing my own happiness and hopefully not
Needing a fresh start.

I think about it though, so I guess that if I ever run out of fresh
Starts and need one, I will make one in my head.

Let go of some part of me and call whatever's left a fresh start even
Though I know it will be a void, a result, simply the sloppy
Seconds of the molestation of innocence that was perpetrated by
Me all by my lonesome.

I've become a psychic in that I know I'll run out of fresh starts and
I know that I'll need to engineer my own, but my psychic abilities
Do not stretch as far as to construct what will have to go to
Welcome the new.

Eh, people don't change.

PEOPLE DON'T CHANGE: AFTERTHOUGHT

I have met and remembered people who are not particularly worth
Remembering.

Therefore, I have completed my study of humans, my
Anthropology studies if you will.

Humans are not easy to remember, as they're engineered to be
Narrow and easily persuaded with fluff and sweetness, though life,
Not the people in said life, avows its horrible stimulus until
Humans are left to deal with falling into or stepping out of their
Own shit—a testament to how "hard" life is, being delimited by
Other people falling into *their* own shit, and leaving humans
Wondering when that tiny window of opportunity passed for them
To step out of their shit and asking how they missed it because
They always do.

COMPLICITY

I believe that complicity
Kills even the best of intentions,
The best of circumstances,
The best of people.

I do not believe in the notion
Of hypocrisy, but I do believe
In the notion of complicity,
The fundament of humans.

I believe I am naturally
Complicit in many things,
Like hating, loving, lust,
Hating and so forth.

Complicity is natural,
But it is evil, and makes me
Acknowledge, subscribe to,
And indulge in things
I disagree with.

CONVERSION

Through the root,
I count three beaten stars
Embedded in the bark.
I take a charred thumb,
And paint blackness
Around my eyes.

I feel the salt of change
Running into the crevices
Of my feet,
From between my feet
To beneath my feet.

AMARBIR SINGH OR: EIGHTEEN YEARS TIME

I stumbled upon,
Among other unexplainable
Things,
In a safe,
The name of my father.

ABOUT THE AUTHOR ... OR POET ... OR WHATEVER

Isaiah M. Williams is a serial entrepreneur, film director, investor, poet, and author from Cleveland, Ohio. Isaiah has founded and served as CEO of multiple companies including The Cottontorch Group, Zinger Media Group, Liven Systems, CLE Group, and The Williams Tie Company. Isaiah also helped to design and lead the nation's first-ever entrepreneurial accelerator for high school students, LightHouse Ohio. He is an avid writer whose works have been published in various media outlets. A book Isaiah wrote about youth entrepreneurship is forthcoming. He is also an author on film history and recently produced, wrote, directed, edited, and scored the film Infinite Regression (2014). He currently studies at Babson College.

www.ingramcontent.com/pod-product-compliance
Lightning Source LLC
Chambersburg PA
CBHW032207040426
42449CB00005B/475